Tides Of The Tender Heart

words for the ones who feel deeply

Aashna Patel

India | USA | UK

Copyright © Aashna Patel
All Rights Reserved.

This book has been self-published with all reasonable efforts taken to make the material error-free by the author. No part of this book shall be used, reproduced in any manner whatsoever without written permission from the author, except in the case of brief quotations embodied in critical articles and reviews.

The Author of this book is solely responsible and liable for its content including but not limited to the views, representations, descriptions, statements, information, opinions, and references ["Content"]. The Content of this book shall not constitute or be construed or deemed to reflect the opinion or expression of the Publisher or Editor. Neither the Publisher nor Editor endorse or approve the Content of this book or guarantee the reliability, accuracy, or completeness of the Content published herein and do not make any representations or warranties of any kind, express or implied, including but not limited to the implied warranties of merchantability, fitness for a particular purpose.

The Publisher and Editor shall not be liable whatsoever...

Made with ❤ on the BookLeaf Publishing Platform
www.bookleafpub.in
www.bookleafpub.com

Dedication

To my family, whose unwavering love and support have been the foundation of my journey,
To my friends, who have walked with me through life's joys and challenges,
To those who have inspired me, challenged me, and encouraged me to explore the depths of my soul,
To the loved ones who have touched my heart and sparked my creativity,
To the memories, both sweet and bittersweet, that have shaped me into who I am today,
I dedicate this book of poetry to you.

Preface

These pages are a reflection of moments quiet, loud, broken, and whole.

Each poem began as a whisper, turning feelings into words I could finally touch.

Here, you'll find pieces of time, stitched together by thought and emotion.

Some verses heal, some question, and some simply exist like breaths between storms.

This collection is not about perfection, but honesty.

It is a journey through love, loss, hope, and everything that lingers in between.

Every line carries a memory, every pause a story untold.

If these words find a place in your heart, then they have found their home.

Thank you for holding my thoughts in your hands.

May you see a little of yourself in these poems.

Acknowledgements

This book would not have come to life without the love, patience, and support of the people around me.

To my family — thank you for being my roots and my reason. Your belief in me has been my quiet strength.

To my friends — for listening, understanding, and inspiring countless lines between laughter and silence.

To everyone who ever shared a story, a moment, or a feeling with me — your presence has shaped my words in ways you may never know.

To the readers — thank you for opening your hearts to my poetry. You give these words meaning beyond the page.

And finally, to my younger self — thank you for feeling deeply and never giving up on expression. You are where every poem began.

Dear Universe,

Thank you for guiding my heart into words.
For every moment that became a poem,
and every silence that taught me to listen.
I'm grateful for the light you placed in these pages
and the strength you placed in me.

With love,
Aashna

1. To my younger self

Hey, little me,
you held onto dreams,
woven from whispers of hope,
each thread a silent prayer.

You danced through storms,
with rain in your hair,
and when the sun broke through,
you wore your scars like art.

You brushed off doubts,
with wings made of hope,
flying higher each time
life knocked you down.

You found beauty in cracks,
and warmth in the cold,
every step a testament
to the stories untold.

I'm proud of you,
for the battles you fought,
for each time you rose,
and the love that you brought.

2. Two Selves

Some days, I wake soft
like sunlight spilling through curtains,
ready to forgive the world
for everything it isn't.

Other days,
I am thunder wrapped in skin,
wanting to tear down the walls
I once built for safety.

I love deeply,
but halfway through the warmth
I wonder if I've given too much,
if love always asks for blood in return.

I crave connection,
yet hide behind silence
afraid that being fully known

means being misunderstood.

Inside me,
hope and fear hold hands,
both whispering, stay.
Both afraid the other will win.

And maybe this is what it means to be alive —
to breathe with a heart split in two,
to ache and heal in the same motion,
to be the wound,
and the hand that tends it.

3. Whispers across the distance

Between us lies a world so wide,
Yet in my heart, you still reside.
No stretch of Earth, no ocean's roar,
Can dim the light we both adore.

Your absence feels like silent rain—
A quiet ache, a gentle pain.
But in that space, your voice I hear,
Whispering love, so calm, so clear.

We share our dreams through midnight skies,
Our laughter echoes, never dies.
Though time may pass & seasons change,
Our souls remain within their range.

Distance is just a fragile wall,
That love & trust will always fall,
For in this bond, so deep, so true,
I carry all of you with me too.

And as the stars begin to fade,
I find your light in every shade.
With every breath, I feel you near,
A compass guiding, crystal clear.

So let the world spin on its track,
In every moment, no turning back.
For intertwined, we'll find our way,
In every dawn, in every day.

4. The Quiet Strength of Friends

They walk with us through shadowed nights,
Illuminate our darkest fights.
In laughter's glow or sorrow's shade,
Their steadfast love will never fade.

When words escape, and tears take flight,
They linger softly, the calming light.
In whispered dreams or silent fears,
They weave our hopes with gentle cheers.

With every moment, memories weave,
A tapestry of what we believe.
Through joy and pain, they choose to stay,
Each heartbeat echoes what words can't say.

In the orchestra of life, they play,
The sweetest notes that guide our way.
A bond unbroken, a truth divine,
Forever yours, forever mine.

5. Girl

A girl, a spark of endless light,
A story woven bright & light,
With dreams that soar beyond the sky;
She builds her world, she dares to fly.

Her laughter rings like morning song,
A melody both pure and strong,
In every step, a rhythm true,
A dance of hope in all she'll do.

She learns, she grows, she leads with grace,
A beacon shining in her place,
With courage deep, she breaks the mold,
A heart of fire, fierce and bold.

In classrooms, fields, or path untold,
Her spirit shines, her story's gold.
A girl, a force, both kind and wise,
The future's light within her eyes.

With every challenge, she will rise,
A tapestry of dreams that ties,
Her vision clear, her purpose grand,
She paints the world with just one hand.

For every doubt, she learns to fight,
A constellation in the night,
A legacy of hope she sows,
In every heart her brilliance glows.

6. Heart of Stone

A heart of stone, so cold, so still,
unmoved by time, untouched by will -
No tear to fall, no warmth to share,
A silent fortress built with care.
Yet deep beneath that stony frame,
A flicker waits, a whispered flame,
For even stones can crack & break
And feel the love they once forsake.
But guarded walls begin to sway
As gentle words find their way.
A thawing touch, a tender hand,
Transform the cold, unyielding land.
The fortress cracks, the silence breaks,
A heart once lost now softly wakes.
From stone to soul, from chill to fire,
Awakens hope, ignites desire.
No longer bound by cold and fear,
Love's gentle light draws ever near
For even hearts once made of stone,

Can find a place to call their own.

7. Birthday

On my own birthday, silence speaks so loud.
A swirling storm beneath a gentle cloud.
Heart-heavy with memories, both bitter and sweet,
A dance of shadows where joy & sorrow meet.
I've carried wounds no one could see,
Hidden battles deep inside of me.
Yet in this stillness, I find my grace.
A fragile smile upon my face.

Loneliness whispers, but so does hope,
Teaching me slowly how to cope.
Each breath a struggle, each heartbeat a fight.
Yet here I am, stepping into the light.
I mourn the moments lost & gone,
But celebrate how far I've come.

On this day that's mine alone
I face the world, though sometimes unknown.
Tears may fall, but so does strength arise.
A quiet power behind my eyes.

On my birthday, raw & true
I hold my heart, I'm breaking through

8. When Death Comes

One day, death will come to me,
Like night that falls across the sea.
It won't be loud, it won't be fast —
Just soft and still, like dreams that pass.

It doesn't knock or make us run,
It waits until our time is done.
And when it comes, it takes our hand,
And leads us to a quiet land.

No more worries, no more pain,
No more walking through the rain.
Just peaceful rest, a gentle end,
Like saying goodbye to a friend.

So I won't fear when death is near,
I'll hold my memories, bright and clear.
For every life must close its eyes,
Like stars that fade from morning skies.

9.

10. The Things We Don't Say

.There were words between us
that never made it to sound
like soft birds,
too fragile for the air.

You'd look at me
and I'd know,
some loves don't need language,
they just exist quietly
between two trembling hearts.

But silence has its own way
of breaking things.
And by the time we spoke,
it was too late
our hearts had already
learned to listen
to the absence.

.

11. Maybe This Is What Love Means

Maybe love isn't fireworks.
Maybe it's the way your name
still feels like home
even when I whisper it to an empty room.

It's in the quiet things
sharing silence without fear,
finding warmth in ordinary moments,
realizing you don't need grand gestures
to feel seen.

You taught me that love isn't about forever,
it's about how deeply it touches you
before it has to leave.

And maybe that's enough
to have loved
so fully,

that even the goodbye
feels sacred

12. What Remains

You don't stop loving someone
just because they're gone.
You just start loving them differently
in memories,
in half-remembered dreams,
in the ache that follows laughter
Some nights,
I still reach for you in my sleep,
and when my hands close on air,
I remind myself—
you were real.
Once, you were here.
And that's enough
for this heart to keep beating.

13. The Kind of Love That Stays

You came like a quiet morning
no fireworks, no thunder,
just the soft certainty of sunlight
finding its way through my tired curtains.

I didn't know love could sound like silence,
like someone staying
when words have failed
and your eyes say, "I understand."

You saw me when I was not a poem,
when my voice cracked on my own name,
when I couldn't find beauty in breathing.
And still, you called me home.

There were days lov hurt
not because it left,
but because it stayed too close
and made me see the parts of me I had buried.

I learned love isn't always soft.
Sometimes it's sitting in the same room
and saying nothing,
but still choosing not to leave.

And even now, when distance
has grown roots between us,
I swear
some nights, I still feel your heartbeat
in the quiet rhythm of my chest.

Because love like that
doesn't end.
It just learns to live
in the spaces we couldn't

14. Flower Field Without Flowers

I used to be full of color
soft winds, wild laughter,
everything alive and reaching for light.

Now I just stand here,
the same earth, the same sky,
but empty in ways words can't touch.

The sun still comes,
but it doesn't warm me the same.
The rain still falls,
but nothing grows from it anymore.

Sometimes I still feel their roots beneath me,
ghosts of what once bloomed.
I still remember the way they smelled,
the way they made me feel alive.

Maybe that's what love does

it leaves, but never really goes.
It stays in the air,
in the spaces that ache quietly.

So I wait not because I believe,
but because I don't know how to stop.
I am the flower field without flowers,
still hoping spring remembers me.

15. Growth hurts soflty

No one tells you that growth
doesn't always look like blooming.
Sometimes it looks like breaking
into silence,
into tears you hide from yourself.

Sometimes it means walking away
from what once felt like home,
even when your heart
still waits by the door.

But one day, you'll notice
your laughter sounds freer,
your steps are lighter,
and the air doesn't sting the same.

Growth isn't loud.
It's the slow, aching miracle
of becoming someone
you never thought you could be

16. Letting Go

I used to think letting go
meant losing
but it's not.
It's remembering without reaching,
caring without clinging.

It's standing in the same place
where everything fell apart
and realizing
you can still breathe here.

Some things aren't meant to stay.
They come to teach you
how love can exist
without possession,
how endings can be
just another form of peace.

And when the wind passes through
what used to be your everything,

you'll understand
you were never meant to hold it forever.
You were meant to hold it
just long enough to grow.

17. It is what it is

some days,
i tell myself those words
just to survive them
it is what it is.

because what else do you say
when things don't turn out
how your heart hoped they would?
when people you loved
forget to love you back?

it's not giving up,
it's just... learning to stop fighting
what's already gone.

maybe this is how life teaches softness
by breaking you gently,
until you learn how to hold pain
without letting it consume you.

it is what it is
not an ending,
just a quiet truth.
and somehow,
in the middle of all that letting go,
i'm still here.
still breathing.
still trying.

18. The Ones Who Leave

some people leave
like seasons
not out of cruelty,
but because their time
was simply done.

and no matter how much you loved,
no matter how hard you tried,
you can't ask summer
to stay in december.

they were real.
you were too.
but some stories end
before you learn how to keep them.

and that's okay.
you carry what mattered.
you let go of what didn't

19. What Time Saw Between Them

time watched them
drift apart
not with anger,
not with storms,
but with a quiet understanding
that some stories
are meant to end softly.

they both carried each other
in different ways
one in silence,
the other in words.
one tried to forget,
the other tried to hold on.
and somewhere between those opposites,
they both learned how to heal.

time saw how pain
became memory,

how memory became peace.
how love,
once too heavy to hold,
became light enough
to live with.

they never said goodbye properly
some hearts don't.
but years passed,
and grief turned into grace.
the sharp edges dulled.
their laughter became a memory,
their memory became warmth.

now, when their thoughts cross paths,
it's not sorrow that stirs

it's something quieter.
a thank you.
a smile.
a soft wish
that the other found peace too.

and time,
ever patient,
whispers to them both:

you loved,
you lost,
you grew.
you became who you were meant to be
because of each other
not despite it.

and that,
in the language of time,
is what love truly means.

20. Misunderstandings

We didn't fall apart in one moment
it happened slowly,
in between small pauses,
in the words we swallowed,
in the way we started saying "it's fine"
when nothing was.

i used to think endings came loudly,
with shouting and doors closing,
but ours came softly
like fading light,
like forgetting what warmth used to feel like.

you thought i stopped caring.
i thought you stopped listening.
and maybe we were both right
in our own ways,
or maybe we were both just tired
of being misunderstood.

i replay the little things sometimes
the look in your eyes
when you thought i didn't notice you drifting,
the moment i realized
i no longer knew how to reach you
without sounding like i was begging.

we were two people
trying to speak love
in different languages,
and neither of us knew
how to translate the hurt.

i wanted you to stay,
but i didn't know how to ask
without breaking my own pride.
and maybe you wanted to stay too,
but didn't know how to say
"i'm still here"
without sounding weak.

so we stayed silent
and silence did what time couldn't.
it turned everything heavy,
everything fragile.
and soon,
we mistook distance for peace.

now, when i think of us,
it's not with anger
just a quiet ache
for what could've been
if only one of us
had said,
i didn't mean to lose you.

maybe in another life
we learn to listen better,
to speak softer,
to stop assuming love
can read minds.

and maybe then,
we won't call it a misunderstanding
we'll call it what it really was:
two hearts trying their best
and missing each other
by just a few words.

21. Crying Isn't Weakness

they told me to be strong
to hold it in,
to keep my voice steady,
to smile through it.

so i did.
i built walls out of silence,
learned to nod instead of break,
learned to laugh when i wanted to scream.

but strength, i've learned,
isn't always about holding it together.
sometimes it's in the moment
your voice shakes,
your eyes fill,
and you let yourself feel
everything you've been avoiding.

crying isn't giving up
it's release.

it's your body saying,
enough pretending.

it's not a sign of weakness,
it's proof that you're still alive
still caring,
still soft in a world
that keeps asking you to be hard.

sometimes tears are the only language
pain knows how to speak.
and when they fall,
they wash away
the weight of unspoken things.

you can be brave and still cry.
you can be healing and still hurt.
you can be strong
and still need a moment to fall apart.

because strength
isn't never breaking
it's breaking
and coming back softer,
wiser,
more open
to the beauty of being human.

so if you need to cry tonight,
do it.
let it pour.
you're not weak
you're real.
and there's nothing braver than that.

22. The Things I Never Say

Some nights,
I whisper to the silence
not for answers,
but for company.
The kind that doesn't ask me to be okay,
just lets me breathe without explaining why
it still hurts.

I've learned that healing
isn't loud.
It's a quiet choosing
to open your eyes on mornings
you swore you wouldn't,
to smile at a world
that once turned its back.

I used to believe strength
was never falling apart.
Now I know
it's the way your trembling hands

still reach for light,
even when darkness feels like home.

Maybe that's what it means to live
to love without guarantee,
to lose without bitterness,
to find pieces of yourself
in the ruins of what you used to be.

And if no one hears your soft survival,
know this:
the universe does.
It takes your pain,
wraps it in dawn,
and turns it into tomorrow.

23. The Way We Drifted

We used to laugh like the world would never end.
Like forever was something we could hold
between shared secrets and late-night talks.
You knew my silence,
I knew your fears,
and that was enough.

We promised
no matter where life took us,
we'd never lose this.
But life has its quiet ways
of pulling people apart
not with anger,
just distance.

No fights.
No last words.
Just slower replies,
then none at all.
And one day,

I realized I was telling stories about us
to people who never knew your name.

Sometimes I still scroll back
to old pictures,
old texts,
old versions of who we were.
You smiled differently back then.
So did I.

I don't hate you for leaving.
I don't blame myself for staying.
Maybe growing up
is learning that not everyone we love
was meant to walk the whole way with us.

But still
when something good happens,
you're the first name my heart calls.
And that's how I know
some friendships don't end,
they just live quietly
in the spaces between memories.

www.ingramcontent.com/pod-product-compliance
Lightning Source LLC
Chambersburg PA
CBHW070038070426
42449CB00012BA/3084